Original title:
Serendipitous Sentiments

Copyright © 2024 Creative Arts Management OÜ
All rights reserved.

Author: Liam Sterling
ISBN HARDBACK: 978-9916-90-718-4
ISBN PAPERBACK: 978-9916-90-719-1

Hues of Happiness in the Unknown

In a world of shifting shades,
We find joy in the unseen,
Whispers of light and laughter,
Painting dreams on canvases keen.

Each step into the unknown,
Brings colors yet to explore,
With every risk, a new tone,
Unlocking happiness's door.

The sky dances with twilight hues,
Stars twinkle in playful delight,
Through shadows of doubt and news,
We discover our inner light.

In silence, the heart sings loud,
Embracing paths that curve and bend,
Among the clouds, we are proud,
Finding bliss in every blend.

Unforeseen Joys

In shadows deep, a light appears,
A whispered laugh, a dance of cheers.
Amid the gray, a bloom unfolds,
New stories weave, as life retolds.

Moments cherished, fleeting grace,
Found in the most unexpected place.
A gentle touch, a soft refrain,
Bringing sunshine after rain.

Fortunate Detours

Winding paths we did not choose,
Lead to treasures, we won't lose.
Through hidden lanes, where secrets hide,
Adventure calls, we take the ride.

With every turn, surprise awaits,
Opening wide, new heavens' gates.
Fortune smiles on roads less known,
In every twist, our dreams have grown.

Guiding Stars of Delight

When night descends, a spark of light,
Guides weary souls to warm their flight.
Each shimmering point, a beacon bright,
Illuminates the heart's delight.

In darkest hours, they stand so tall,
Whispers of hope through the silent call.
Together we shine, like constellations,
In harmony with our aspirations.

Happy Coincidences

A chance encounter, eyes that meet,
Fate's gentle hand in every beat.
A serendipitous twist of fate,
Crafts beautiful stories we celebrate.

Laughter echoes in the air,
Connections spark with tender care.
Moments shared, a joyful dance,
Life's whims lead us to romance.

Mystical Trails of Delight

In the forest where shadows play,
Magic dances in light's soft sway.
Whispers carry on the breeze,
Nature's secrets, hearts to please.

Golden leaves beneath our feet,
Every step, a rhythmic beat.
Paths of wonder, mysteries wait,
In each moment, love and fate.

Whispers of Fortunate Chance

Beneath the stars, we chance to meet,
In quiet corners, hearts find their beat.
Serendipity in every glance,
Life unfolds in a fortunate dance.

Echoes of laughter fill the night,
In serendipity, there's pure delight.
Fortune favors those who dare,
To seek the moments floating in air.

Unseen Threads of Destiny

Woven tightly, unseen strands,
Guiding us with gentle hands.
By fate's design, we intertwine,
In the tapestry, our stories shine.

Paths converge, like rivers flow,
In the fabric, love will grow.
Stars align, our futures blend,
In every journey, we transcend.

Songs of Lucky Encounters

Melodies drift on a soulful breeze,
Each note carries a moment to seize.
Harmonies rise as souls align,
In lucky meetings, destinies twine.

Voices blend in sweet refrain,
Unlikely friendships, love's gentle gain.
In serendipitous moments we find,
The songs of life that fill the mind.

Fortunate Fumbles in Love

In the dance of chance we glide,
With stumbles that our hearts can hide.
A laugh, a glance, we miss the mark,
Yet still, we find our way through dark.

Wounds of pride softly heal,
In tender moments, we reveal.
Fortune favors the bold we say,
Love's foolish fumbles light the way.

Glimmers of Joy in Shadows

Beneath the clouds, faint lights will gleam,
Whispers of hope, like a waking dream.
In the depths, where sorrows creep,
A spark ignites, our souls to keep.

Joy blooms bright in hidden places,
Flickers of laughter on weary faces.
In shadows deep, a lesson learned,
Through trials, brighter paths are turned.

Unfolding Stories of Delight

Every moment, a tale to weave,
In laughter and love, we dare to believe.
Pages turn, new chapters arise,
With every heartbeat, new worlds surprise.

In shared smiles, our spirits soar,
Together we dance, forevermore.
Unfurling dreams, a tapestry spun,
Life's joyful stories have just begun.

Silent Echoes of Change

In whispers soft, the winds will sigh,
The old must fade for the new to fly.
A quiet shift, a gentle hand,
With each heartbeat, we understand.

Echoes faint from the past resound,
In silence, growth and hope abound.
Embrace the change, let go the pain,
In stillness, we find our strength to reign.

Serendipity's Gentle Touch

In shadows soft, fate calls us near,
A whisper sweet, the heart can hear.
Moments weave, like threads of gold,
In gentle touch, new stories told.

A chance encounter, smiles ignite,
Paths cross in the soft moonlight.
The world expands, horizons shift,
In serendipity, we find our gift.

Dreams Unfolding Unexpectedly

In quiet nights, visions arise,
Glimmers bright behind closed eyes.
Layered wishes, softly spun,
Beneath the stars, dreams have begun.

Each twist and turn, surprise awaits,
An open door, a chance that fates.
Wings unfurl, to soar and glide,
In dreams unfolding, we shall ride.

Collisions of Joy

Laughter dances, hearts collide,
In playful chaos, side by side.
Moments spark like stars above,
In joyful crashes, we find love.

The melody of life plays loud,
In vibrant hues, we stand so proud.
Surprise embraced, in each delight,
Collisions of joy, pure and bright.

The Radiance of Fortunate Happenstance

In chance encounters, fate takes flight,
Guiding us toward the radiant light.
Each twist of fate, a dance divine,
In happenstance, our hearts align.

Moments woven, threads unseen,
A tapestry of what could be.
The universe smiles; we take a chance,
In fortunate paths, we found romance.

Raindrops of Unforeseen Delight

Softly they fall, whispers of grace,
Dancing on rooftops, a delicate lace.
Each droplet holds secrets, hidden and bright,
A world awakens with cheer and delight.

Children in puddles, laughter does soar,
Joy in each splash, wanting nothing more.
Nature hums softly, a sweet serenade,
In moments like these, our worries do fade.

Glimmers of Unstaged Hearts

In the quiet corners where shadows reside,
Glimmers of feelings no longer can hide.
Eyes meet like stars in a twilight dance,
Hearts speak in silence, igniting romance.

A touch, a smile, the world fades away,
Unsure yet knowing, come what may.
Unscripted stories, where love finds its way,
In glimmers of moments that promise to stay.

The Magic of the Unpredictable

Winds whisper secrets through branches above,
Life takes its turns, a tapestry of love.
Moments unexpected, a spark in the night,
Bring forth the magic, igniting delight.

Paths intertwining, lost in the flow,
Each twist, each turn, leads to the glow.
Embrace the unknown, let go of the reigns,
In the dance of the moment, joy always reigns.

Threads of Fate Intertwined

In a tapestry woven, stories unfold,
Threads of our fates, both timid and bold.
Each stitch a journey, a moment in time,
Connected in ways that feel so sublime.

When paths cross gently, like stars in the sky,
We weave together, as dreams wander by.
Inknots of our lives, a beautiful sign,
In threads of fate, our hearts intertwine.

Happenstance and Happiness

In the twist of fate we find,
A spark ignites, our hearts entwined.
Through chance encounters, joy can rise,
In whispered dreams and sweet surprise.

Moments merge, like rivers flow,
Unexpected paths begin to show.
Laughter dances in the air,
Happenstance leads us everywhere.

With every turn, a chance to see,
The beauty in simplicity.
When serendipity strikes near,
Happiness blooms, forever clear.

Love by Chance's Design

A casual glance, our eyes collide,
In crowded rooms, we're drawn inside.
By fate's own hand, our stories blend,
Love by chance, we dare to send.

Winding paths and tangled ties,
Whispers soft, like tender sighs.
In moments lost, we find our place,
By chance's design, our hearts embrace.

With every twist, a dance anew,
Together in life's vibrant hue.
A tapestry of love's delight,
By chance we shine, forever bright.

The Light of Unanticipated Moments

In shadows cast by fleeting time,
Unplanned encounters, sense sublime.
A laugh, a glance, it starts to spark,
The light of joy ignites the dark.

With every breath, we're unprepared,
For gifts that life has freely shared.
A serendipitous embrace,
Reveals the warmth of love's true face.

Unexpected turns lead us here,
To cherish all that feels so near.
In this embrace of happenstance,
We find a love that's more than chance.

Radiance in Randomness

In chaos blooms a gentle grace,
Each twist and turn, a warm embrace.
From random acts, love's whispers grow,
Radiance shines from chance's glow.

Through winding roads, we stumble on,
In fleeting moments, hearts are drawn.
An open mind, a willing heart,
From randomness, we won't depart.

With every laugh that breaks the night,
We celebrate the pure delight.
In every glance, a spark ignites,
Radiance blooms in chance-filled nights.

Life's Beautiful Mishaps

A stumble here, a fall from grace,
Each misstep brings a smile to face.
The turns in life, they twist and bend,
In every flaw, new paths extend.

With every crack, the light streams in,
In brokenness, there hides a grin.
A laugh can bloom from pain's embrace,
In life's great dance, we find our place.

Embracing the Uncertain

In shadows cast by doubt and fear,
We learn to tread where paths aren't clear.
The winds may whisper tales of change,
In chaos lies a chance to range.

With every step, the heart takes flight,
Guided by stars that spark the night.
We hold on tight, we let love steer,
Embracing all that feels so near.

Laughs in the Laps of Fate

When echoes ring of chance and cheer,
We find our joy, we hold it dear.
A jest unwinds in moments brief,
In laughter's arms, we find relief.

The fates may tease, they twist and play,
Yet smiles are here to light the way.
In playful jabs, we dance and sway,
Finding joy in every day.

Swaying to the Rhythm of Surprise

A sudden twist, a sway, a turn,
In life's great dance, we learn to yearn.
With open hearts, we greet the new,
Each moment brings a vibrant hue.

In every shock, a chance to grow,
The path awaits for us to glow.
So let us dance through each surprise,
Finding grace in life's disguise.

When Time Stands Still

In a whisper, the clock surrenders,
Moments linger like autumn leaves.
Shadows dance, time gently suspends,
Echoes of dreams softly weave.

Eyes closed, the world falls away,
Breath holds the secrets of night.
Fleeting seconds refuse to decay,
In stillness, we find our light.

Curious Paths Crossed

On winding roads in the fading glow,
Two souls wander, hearts unconfined.
Whispers of fate in the softest flow,
In silence, their destinies aligned.

Footsteps meet on a bridge of chance,
Time suspends in a hushed embrace.
A fleeting moment, a tender glance,
Two worlds merge in this sacred space.

Euphoria in the Unexpected

A sudden laugh in a crowded room,
Hearts awaken to joy's sweet thrill.
Moments bloom, dispelling the gloom,
In the chaos, solace we instill.

Fleeting smiles in twilight's grasp,
Uncharted paths ignite the heart.
With every touch, we dare to clasp,
Euphoria's dance, a work of art.

The Beauty of Unforeseen Journeys

Beyond horizons where dreams collide,
Unmapped roads weave tales anew.
In every step, the heart's wild ride,
Truths unravel in shades of blue.

With courage as our guiding star,
Together we traverse the night.
Transforming fears into a scar,
In unforeseen journeys, we find light.

When Chance Meets the Heart

A glance across the crowded room,
Two souls collide in silent bloom.
Fate weaves threads of random chance,
In whispered words, they dare to dance.

Moments drift like autumn leaves,
Carried forth on gentle eves.
Hearts entwined in serendipity,
Found in sweet simplicity.

Paths may cross in hidden ways,
In fleeting smiles, the heart obeys.
Beneath the stars, a spark ignites,
As dreams unite on quiet nights.

A chance encounter, fate's embrace,
Lost in time, yet found in space.
In every heartbeat quietly shared,
Love's sweet magic, truth declared.

Fortunes in the Flicker of Eyes

In gazes held, the world ignites,
Fortunes found in playful flights.
A moment caught, electric spark,
Life's soft whispers kindling dark.

Like shadows dancing on the wall,
Eyes reveal, hearts heed the call.
In laughter shared, a fortune gleams,
A treasure born from fleeting dreams.

The flicker speaks of places bright,
Where wishes bloom and hearts take flight.
In every glance, a tale unfolds,
A magic deep, a bond of gold.

A glance that lingers in the night,
Fortunes bloom with pure delight.
Each spark ignites the soul anew,
In eyes that dance, old skies turn blue.

Gifts Wrapped in Surprise

Life's wrapped moments, soft and dear,
A gentle touch, a subtle cheer.
In every pause, a gift awaits,
The simple joys that love creates.

Surprises bloom like flowers in spring,
A whispered wish, the heart takes wing.
Each twist and turn, a story spun,
In every shadow, joy begun.

Unseen blessings fill the air,
In laughter shared, in tender care.
With every dawn, the gift of hope,
In unexpected ways, we learn to cope.

Life's mysteries wrapped up in grace,
In every smile, a warm embrace.
Each precious moment we unveil,
Becomes a treasure in love's tale.

Echoes of Joyful Coincidence

Whispers linger in the breeze,
Joyful echoes, worlds at ease.
Each twist of fate a song that plays,
In serendipity's warm embrace.

A chance encounter, laughter's ring,
Fortunes born on fleeting wing.
In moments shared, bright spirits soar,
Life's delightful dance, forevermore.

Rays of sunshine through the trees,
Every glance a gentle tease.
In the tapestry of chance we weave,
Echoes linger, hearts believe.

The magic found in random ties,
Brings bright delight, a sweet surprise.
In love's reflection, fate's soft song,
Together, where we all belong.

Whimsical Wonders of Life

In gardens where the daisies sway,
Wonder blooms in bright array.
Butterflies dance on gentle breeze,
The world unfolds with perfect ease.

Laughter sparkles in the sun,
Every heart has just begun.
Moments sweet like honey flow,
In the light, our spirits glow.

Clouds drift in a dreamy race,
Magic finds a cozy space.
With every step, new sights to find,
In this realm, our souls unwind.

Let joy paint the skies so clear,
Side by side, with those we hold dear.
Adventure waits on every street,
In life's wonders, we are complete.

Shadows of Unplanned Bliss

In twilight's soft and gentle shade,
Unexpected paths are laid.
Fleeting moments weave a tapestry,
In shadows of sweet history.

Laughter echoes in the night,
Guided by the moon's soft light.
Dreams unfold with every glance,
In the dark, we find romance.

Starlit skies weave stories bold,
Whispers of the heart unfold.
Each step taken, hand in hand,
In this dance, we understand.

Memories linger, softly kissed,
In unplanned bliss, we exist.
Life unfurls, a mystery,
In every shade, our hearts fly free.

An Array of Happy Happenings

From morning's light to evening's glow,
In every heart, a joy will grow.
Smiles exchanged, a warm embrace,
In life's dance, we find our place.

Unexpected friends we meet,
With laughter rich and moments sweet.
In simple acts, our spirits soar,
In shared kindness, we find more.

Every sunrise is a chance,
To cherish life and join the dance.
A touch, a word, a glance, a song,
An array of joys to carry along.

With every heartbeat, we align,
In happy happenings, we shine.
Life's a tapestry, finely spun,
Together, we have just begun.

Serendipity in Every Breath

In moments soft, where dreams collide,
Serendipity, our faithful guide.
With every breath, a story shared,
In unexpected ways, we're paired.

Wandering through paths unknown,
In gentle whispers, love is grown.
Chance encounters light the way,
In twilight's glow, we wish to stay.

Each heartbeat echoes fate's sweet call,
In the dance of life, we risk it all.
Together weaving moments pure,
In serendipity, we're sure.

With open hearts and open eyes,
We find our fortune in the skies.
In every breath, a chance to see,
The magic that unfurls, so free.

Hidden Gems of the Heart

In whispers soft, secrets lie,
Treasures hidden, where dreams fly.
A gentle touch, a knowing glance,
Awakens souls in sweet romance.

Through tangled paths we often roam,
In quiet corners, we find home.
The heart's true gems, we hold so dear,
In shared moments, love draws near.

Each laugh and tear, a thread we weave,
In the tapestry, we believe.
Fleeting time, yet forever stays,
In hidden gems, love's light displays.

Beneath the stars, the heart's embrace,
Unveiling dreams in sacred space.
Together we shine, a radiant art,
With every beat, hidden gems of heart.

Unraveled Threads of Luck

In tangled skeins, our destinies twist,
A dance of fate, in shadows missed.
With every turn, we seek the thread,
That binds us close, where fortunes spread.

A chance encounter, a fleeting smile,
Change the course of life's long mile.
Unraveled dreams, yet still we find,
The golden strands that fate designed.

In laughter's glow, or teardrops' fall,
We gather strength, through it all.
Every moment, a woven part,
In the grand design of the heart.

Embrace the twist, the wild unknown,
In every stumble, seeds are sown.
With open arms, we greet our luck,
In the dance of life's unraveled luck.

Laughter in the Unlikely

Amidst the storms of daily strife,
We find a spark that brings us life.
In unexpected places, joy will bloom,
Turning dark corners into bright rooms.

A child's giggle, a friend's embrace,
Moments that time cannot erase.
Through trials faced and battles fought,
Laughter echoes, all joy sought.

In the unlikeliest of times, we see,
A world alive with possibility.
With hearts unburdened, we take flight,
Laughter guides us, a beacon bright.

So let us cherish every chance,
To dance with joy, to laugh and prance.
In the tapestry of life's design,
Laughter shines, forever divine.

Curious Turns of Fate

In winding roads where shadows play,
Curious turns lead us astray.
A twist of chance, a fleeting flight,
Shapes a tomorrow from endless night.

A serendipitous meeting, a glance,
Life shifts gently, as if in a dance.
Paths converge, like rivers meet,
Fate's hands guiding, swift and fleet.

Through whispers of what might have been,
Adventure calls, our hearts to win.
In moments strange, we find our way,
Curious turns, brightening the day.

Let us embrace the unexpected,
For in those twists, life is reflected.
With open hearts, we navigate,
The curious turns that shape our fate.

Kisses from the Unexpected

In shadows where the soft winds play,
A whisper blooms in bright dismay.
A touch of fate, it sweeps along,
In tender moments, we belong.

Surprise alights like morning's dew,
With every smile, the world feels new.
Hearts collide in gentle sighs,
The magic lives in secret eyes.

Beneath the stars, our laughter swells,
In hidden corners, love compels.
Each glance exchanged, a sweet embrace,
Kisses borne from time and space.

In unexpected trails we dance,
With every heartbeat, a second chance.
Life's sweetest gift, the unplanned kiss,
In fleeting moments, we find bliss.

Fleeting Glances of Fortune

Across the room, a glance does dart,
A spark ignites within the heart.
Fortune's smile, a touch so rare,
In fleeting looks, we dare to share.

Moments lost in time's embrace,
As chance and luck begin to chase.
A silent nod, a knowing wink,
In stolen glances, spirits link.

Paths intertwine like threads of gold,
In every gaze, a story told.
Fortune favors those who see,
The beauty in uncertainty.

With every spark, the magic grows,
In cosmic dance that fate bestows.
These fleeting looks, our hearts collide,
In chance encounters, love's pure tide.

Journeys Beyond the Horizon

With every step, new landscapes call,
Adventures wait beyond the fall.
The sun will rise, a compass true,
Leading hearts toward skies so blue.

Mountains high and valleys wide,
In every shadow, dreams abide.
Beneath the stars, our spirits roam,
Journeys made, we find our home.

Through rivers deep and forests vast,
Each moment lived, a spell is cast.
With hands held tight, we wander free,
Unraveling life's great mystery.

Horizons beckon, sails unfurl,
As waves of hope begin to swirl.
With open hearts, we dare to soar,
Journeys await, forevermore.

Daydreams of the Sudden

In quiet corners, thoughts take flight,
Exploring realms of soft twilight.
Daydreams drift through endless skies,
Where whispers echo and hope flies.

The sudden spark of fleeting bliss,
In every thought, a gentle kiss.
Time collapses in a breath,
In reveries of life and death.

Unexpected paths through haze do weave,
In dreams, the mind learns to believe.
With every glance and subtle sway,
The heart finds magic, come what may.

Awake, asleep, in moments lost,
It's in these daydreams we find cost.
For life is but a canvas bright,
With sudden strokes of love and light.

Threads of Fortune

In the loom of life we weave,
Threads of hope, dreams to achieve.
Each color bright, stories told,
Fate's gentle hand, a dance bold.

In shadows cast, fortunes blend,
Paths entwined, they twist and bend.
To the unknown, we take flight,
Trusting the thread, guiding light.

Through trials faced, laughter shared,
In every stitch, love declared.
Together we weave, hearts aligned,
A tapestry rich, forever defined.

In threads of fortune, fate's embrace,
We find our strength, a sacred space.
With every twist, a chance to grow,
In this grand design, let love flow.

The Unplanned Symphony

In a world of notes unplayed,
Life's symphony, beautifully laid.
Each moment strikes, a chord so rare,
Unplanned rhythms fill the air.

Harmony found in chaos bright,
Melodies dance in soft moonlight.
With every chance, we take a leap,
In melodies lost, secrets keep.

From whispered tones, new dreams arise,
Unexpected joys, surprise the skies.
Together we play, hearts in sync,
In this grand score, we learn to think.

Unplanned symphony, hearts inspired,
In each crescendo, we are wired.
Let go of scripts, embrace the sound,
In every note, true love is found.

Starlit Surprises

Under the stars, dreams ignite,
Whispers of wonder through the night.
Each twinkle tells tales of old,
Starlit surprises, dreams unfold.

Moonlit paths we wander too,
In cosmic dance, me and you.
Galaxies spin, love's embrace,
With every glance, we find our place.

In hidden corners, wishes bloom,
Laughter carries, lights the gloom.
Stardust trails, sparkles in flight,
Holding secrets of the night.

We chase the shadows, hearts aligned,
In starlit moments, joy defined.
With every spark, a promise lies,
Embracing love, starlit skies.

Moments of Pure Magic

In fleeting glances, magic grows,
Moments captured, life bestows.
With every breath, a spell we cast,
In the ordinary, shadows past.

Every heartbeat, a dance divine,
Weaving stories, yours and mine.
A laugh, a tear, the magic swells,
In whispered secrets, our heart tells.

Through misty mornings, dawn awakes,
Moments shine, the world it makes.
In simple joys, we find our grace,
Pure magic dwells in every space.

Holding on to fragments bright,
In moments cherished, pure delight.
Life's tapestry, woven with care,
Magic lingers, always there.

Starlit Pathways of Discovery

Underneath the vast night sky,
Whispers of dreams gently float by.
Each step takes us deeper still,
Curious hearts, we bend to will.

Twinkling lights guide our way,
In the dark, where shadows play.
Every corner holds a tale,
Through the starlit paths we sail.

Secrets hidden in the glow,
What we seek begins to show.
Footprints left in silvery dust,
Paths of wonder are a must.

With each star, a wish takes flight,
In this dance of pure delight.
Together we'll brave the unknown,
In starlit pathways, we have grown.

Spontaneous Breaths of Joy

Laughter echoes in the air,
Moments caught without a care.
Surprise awaits on every street,
Life's sweet pleasures, pure and neat.

A child's giggle, a fleeting glance,
In every heartbeat, we find chance.
Spontaneous joy in simple things,
In the breeze, our spirit sings.

Bubbles rising, colors bright,
Chasing sunsets, chasing light.
With every smile, a spark we share,
In spontaneous breaths, we dare.

Together we dance in the sun,
Underneath the sky, we run.
Life's sweetest moments weave and blend,
In joyous breaths, our souls extend.

Whispers of Fortuitous Hearts

In the shadows where dreams softly sigh,
Two souls converge, beneath the twilight sky.
With laughter woven in the gentle night,
Whispers of fate dance in candlelight.

Beneath the stars, their secrets intertwine,
Every heartbeat sings, a sweet design.
In serendipity, their spirits soar,
Together they find what they couldn't before.

A touch of fate brings smiles to their grace,
In every moment, a warm embrace.
Through the chaos, they find their way,
Two hearts aligned, come what may.

As destiny nudges with tender hands,
They walk together, where love expands.
In whispers soft, they bravely start,
Crafting their tale, two fortuitous hearts.

Unexpected Sunbeams

Amidst the clouds where shadows lay low,
A glow emerges, starting to show.
With every smile, the dawn breaks clear,
Happiness blooms, as hope draws near.

A chance encounter on a rainy day,
Brightens the heart in a magical way.
As laughter dances on the breeze,
They share their stories with perfect ease.

In moments fleeting, joy takes flight,
Painting their world in colors so bright.
Each sunbeam whispers of dreams anew,
Illuminating paths where love breaks through.

With every glance, the sun shines more,
Unexpected warmth they both adore.
In every heartbeat, a promise found,
In life's surprises, their hearts are bound.

Chance Encounters in Twilight

As dusk descends, the world grows still,
Fleeting faces spark an unseen thrill.
In twilight's arms, two strangers meet,
Fate's tapestry woven, with threads so sweet.

With laughter shared at a corner café,
Two worlds collide in a beautiful way.
Eyes shimmering bright, they find their tune,
Under the watchful gaze of the moon.

A shared glance ignites a flame,
In gentle whispers, they speak no name.
Every moment holds a breathless art,
An echo of souls that yearn to part.

What once was happenstance, now feels profound,
In the dance of twilight, their hearts resound.
In chance encounters, magic unfurls,
As secrets emerge in the softest swirls.

The Dance of Happy Accidents

In the chaos of life, a rhythm grows,
Two wanderers find what nobody knows.
With every stumble, a miracle springs,
A serendipitous waltz that fate sings.

Through blunders sweet, they find their way,
Laughter and love in a bright display.
Every bump in the road leads to dreams,
In the dance of life, joy brightly beams.

They twirl through mishaps with grace in their hearts,
Each spin and laugh, a masterpiece starts.
In the embrace of the unpredictable night,
Happy accidents helped them take flight.

Together they sway, hand in hand,
With every step, they make their stand.
In this dance, they truly belong,
Two souls entwined in a beautiful song.

Chasing Moments of Magic

In twilight whispers, dreams unfurl,
Through shadows cast, a hidden pearl.
Each fleeting glance, a spark ignites,
Chasing moments, we reach new heights.

With open hearts, we dare to soar,
Embracing magic at every door.
The stars above, they guide our way,
In the night's embrace, we wish to stay.

A dance of colors, a canvas bright,
Painting memories in fading light.
With laughter's echo, we laugh and play,
Chasing magic, come what may.

In every heartbeat, the world ignites,
Chasing moments through endless nights.
Together we wander, hand in hand,
In this realm where dreams expand.

Spirited Adventures of the Heart

In the quiet morn, spirits arise,
With every heartbeat, the world flies.
Across the hills, we laugh and run,
Chasing adventures in the sun.

With open eyes, we seek the thrill,
Through valleys deep, we find our will.
The whispers of love in every breeze,
A symphony played among the trees.

Through winding paths, our laughter swells,
In stories shared, the heart compels.
From mountain tops to oceans wide,
Spirited journeys, love as our guide.

Together we wander, wild and free,
In the dance of life, just you and me.
Embracing moments that tear apart,
These spirited adventures of the heart.

A Song for the Undesigned

In shadows deep, we find our tune,
A song for hearts that break too soon.
Each note a tear, each chord a sigh,
For every dream that dared to fly.

With whispers soft, we write our fate,
In melodies that resonate.
Though unrefined, our voices rise,
A harmony born from our goodbyes.

In tangled lines, we weave our song,
For every moment we felt wrong.
Yet in the pain, a beauty lies,
A song for souls who seek the skies.

Through trials faced, we stand as one,
Singing of battles that must be won.
In imperfections, we find our light,
A song for the undesigned takes flight.

Nurtured by Nebulous Fate

In the fabric of time, we softly tread,
Nurtured by dreams that dance in our head.
With threads of hope, we stitch our way,
Through nebulous paths where shadows play.

In silken whispers, the future calls,
While destiny dances behind the walls.
In moments crafted by chance and grace,
Nurtured by fate, we find our place.

With stars above, our journey sparkles,
On winding roads where our heart marvels.
Each step we take, a story unfolds,
In the warmth of fate, our life is told.

Through the unknown, we bravely roam,
In nebulous realms, we make our home.
Together in dreams, with love as our state,
Nurtured forever by nebulous fate.

Echoes of Lucky Hearts

In a quiet nook, love does bloom,
Whispers of fate in the glowing room.
Stars align in a soft embrace,
Echoes of laughter, a timeless trace.

With every glance, a spark ignites,
Filling the world with warm delights.
Paths once diverged, now intertwined,
Lucky hearts, forever aligned.

Through storms and shadows, hand in hand,
Together we weave a golden strand.
Every heartbeat, a sweet refrain,
Echoes of love, a gentle gain.

As the days turn and seasons flow,
In this journey, together we grow.
With echoes ringing, our spirits soar,
Lucky hearts, forevermore.

Discovering Bliss in the Ordinary

Amidst the chaos, a moment breathes,
In simple sights, true joy weaves.
A cup of tea, sun-kissed light,
Finding bliss in the soft, sweet night.

Footsteps crunch on autumn leaves,
A child's laughter, the heart believes.
In everyday spaces, magic hides,
Discovering bliss where life resides.

Glimpses of beauty in mundane scenes,
Whispers of wonders in everyday dreams.
Embracing the calm in a simple tune,
Joy dances lightly like a silver moon.

In each small gesture, in every glance,
Ordinary moments invite us to dance.
Finding delight in the small and grand,
Life's true treasure, right at hand.

Tides of Unexpected Affection

Like waves crashing on the shore,
Unexpected love opens the door.
A glance across a bustling street,
Tides of feelings, warm and sweet.

In the quiet of a shared smile,
Hearts align, if just for a while.
Every heartbeat, a novel key,
Unlocking doors to what could be.

Beneath the stars, stories unfold,
Adventures waiting, brave and bold.
In fleeting moments, connections rise,
Tides of affection under moonlit skies.

As seasons change and timelines shift,
Love's gentle pull becomes a gift.
With every tide, we come to see,
Unexpected paths lead to harmony.

Embracing the Unanticipated

Life's twists and turns, a winding road,
Embracing changes, lightens the load.
In every detour, a lesson found,
Unanticipated joy knows no bound.

With open hearts, we face the new,
Each surprise brings colors, fresh and true.
In moments unplanned, we find our way,
Embracing the magic of each bright day.

As laughter spills from the unforeseen,
We celebrate what has never been.
A dance with fate, a playful chance,
Unanticipated love takes us to a trance.

Through challenges faced, and dreams set free,
Life unfolds like a wild, vast sea.
In every wave, a story spins,
Embracing each moment, the journey begins.

Destined Awakenings

In the quiet dawn we rise,
A gentle whisper in the skies.
Fates align like stars above,
Awakening the need for love.

As the sun breaks forth its light,
Hope unfurls, banishing night.
We walk the path that fate has drawn,
Together, facing each new dawn.

With every step, the world expands,
Guided by unseen hands.
In the garden of our dreams,
We find joy in simple themes.

Bound by threads of destiny,
We embrace our mystery.
Hand in hand, we chase the day,
In our hearts, we find the way.

Skylines of Surprising Affection

Underneath the city lights,
Hearts collide on starry nights.
In the whispers of the breeze,
We discover sweet unease.

Skyscrapers reach, but love ascends,
In unexpected ways, it bends.
Glimmers dance in beating hearts,
As daylight fades and magic starts.

Moments shared in fleeting glances,
Life is woven with its chances.
Every laugh, each softer sigh,
Builds the skyline of the sky.

Together we will brave the storm,
In embrace, we find our form.
With every step, a brand-new view,
Surprising, tender, always true.

The Poetry of Spontaneous Moments

In a blink, a spark ignites,
Life unfolds in sheer delights.
A laugh erupts, a dance ensues,
Spontaneity's vibrant hues.

Time stands still, the world fades back,
Embracing joy, we find the track.
Unwritten tales in fleeting bliss,
Moments cherished, none to miss.

Echoes of laughter fill the air,
Holding hands, we have a prayer.
A glance, a wink, a shared embrace,
In each heartbeat, we find our place.

Unplanned paths are where we roam,
Carving memories, feeling home.
Each second, a verse to create,
In spontaneity, we navigate.

Beautiful Messes of Fate

Amidst the chaos, beauty brews,
In tangled threads, we find our muse.
Life's palette splashed with joyful strife,
Crafting art from the simplest life.

Fate's hand paints with vibrant brush,
In a moment, dreams may crush.
Yet from the ruin, hope does rise,
Revealing strength in our disguise.

Mistakes turn into lessons learned,
In every tear, a fire burned.
We embrace the wild and the raw,
In messy moments, we find the law.

So let us dance through life's unknown,
In beautifully crafted, chaotic tone.
With every step, embrace the grace,
In messiness, we find our place.

The Art of Happy Discoveries

In the quiet of the morning light,
A whisper calls, a spark ignites.
Amid the shadows, treasures shine,
A world of wonder, yours and mine.

With every step, a tale unfolds,
A hidden gem, a story told.
The heart expands, the spirit soars,
In simple joys, adventure pours.

Curiosity, a guiding star,
Leading us near and far.
Through paths untraveled, unmarked trails,
We find our way, as laughter sails.

In every glance, a chance to see,
The beauty in what's wild and free.
Discoveries dance like fireflies,
Illuminating the darkest skies.

Joys that Caught Me Unawares

A sudden laugh, a fleeting glance,
Moments gifted, a serendipitous chance.
In simple things, the heart does swell,
A secret joy that words can't tell.

A child's giggle, a friend's kind word,
The sweetest song, softly heard.
In bustling days, small wonders sneak,
A timeless smile, that words can't speak.

The sun's warm kiss, a gentle breeze,
Nature's gifts put my mind at ease.
In the bloom of spring, life's charms appear,
Joys that catch me, always near.

Moments weave, life's tapestry,
Hidden blessings, a symphony.
Through trials faced, such beauty grows,
In unexpected ways, love bestows.

Navigating Through Sweet Mysteries

In twilight's hush, the stars align,
Whispers of fate, a tale divine.
Paths entwined, in shadows we roam,
Each twist and turn, leads us home.

Questions linger, as night draws near,
Answers hidden, yet feel so clear.
In every silence, secrets thrive,
The pulse of life, keeps dreams alive.

With every heartbeat, a choice to make,
To trust the road, with steps we take.
Through fog and doubt, we'll find our way,
Embracing the dawn, of a brand new day.

Embrace the unknown, let courage reign,
In sweet mysteries, there's no disdain.
In the dance of fate, we'll surely find,
Life's sweetest moments; hearts entwined.

The Beauty of Happy Mistakes

In tangled threads, life's weave unfolds,
A splash of color, a story told.
What seems askew may lead to grace,
In happy mistakes, we find our place.

With gentle laughter, we rise again,
Each misstep a lesson, not a strain.
In broken lines, new art begins,
From flaws embraced, true beauty wins.

Through slips and fumbles, we learn and grow,
In every stumble, a chance to glow.
With open hearts, the world we face,
Each blunder's gift, a warm embrace.

So let us dance through life's sweet chance,
In every misstep, find our dance.
For in the end, the truth remains,
The beauty of life is in the strains.

Sweet Serendipity in the Air

A whisper of chance floats by,
Breezes dance with a gentle sigh.
Moments collide, hearts align,
In this spark, our souls entwine.

The sun breaks through the cloudy gray,
With every step, we find our way.
Laughter flows like sweet champagne,
In these moments, joy remains.

Unplanned nights under starlit skies,
Where secrets bloom and hope replies.
In every glance, a spark is found,
Sweet serendipity surrounds.

Together we weave our dreams so bright,
Shadows fade in the warm twilight.
Hand in hand, we're bravely bold,
In this tale, our love unfolds.

Chance's Gentle Hands

Through the maze of life's design,
Chance's hands guide, they intertwine.
With every turn, a thrill prevails,
In unexpected twists, love sails.

The clock ticks softly, not in haste,
Moments cherished, none laid waste.
With laughter's echo in the air,
We find ourselves without a care.

A fleeting glance, a smile exchanged,
In this dance, our paths are changed.
With gentle whispers of the night,
We embrace the soft delight.

With every step, the world feels new,
Chance's hands guide me to you.
In the story of fate's sweet grant,
Love blooms where we both enchant.

Love's Unplanned Journey

On winding roads, we stumbled near,
In laughter's glow, we conquered fear.
Each turn a chance, each mile a gift,
In love's embrace, our spirits lift.

Moments fleeting, yet so profound,
Through the chaos, a peace is found.
Two souls wandering, side by side,
In this journey, our hearts abide.

The map is blurred, yet we still roam,
In every heartbeat, we feel at home.
Not by design, nor charted course,
But by love's magic, we find our source.

With open hearts and daring minds,
In unplanned paths, true love unwinds.
Together we chase the stars above,
In every step, we choose our love.

A Tapestry of Happy Happenstance

Threads of fate weave dreams so bright,
In the tapestry of soft moonlight.
Patterns formed through chance and grace,
In every stitch, we find our place.

Laughter melds with starlit skies,
In serendipity, our spirits rise.
Unexpected joys, they fill the air,
In every heartbeat, we find we care.

Colors swirl in vibrant hues,
With each new day, we chase our muse.
Through twists and turns, we gently sway,
In every moment, love finds a way.

A tapestry rich with life and song,
In precious threads, we both belong.
Together we craft our sweet romance,
In this dance of happy happenstance.

Embraces in Unexpected Places

In crowded rooms where shadows play,
A tender touch can light the way.
Moments pause, hearts dive deep,
In silent whispers, promises keep.

The laughter shared, a fleeting glance,
Two souls entwined in serendipity's dance.
A brush of hands, a spark ignites,
In every corner, warmth invites.

Beneath the stars, where dreams unfold,
Emotions bloom, stories told.
Fragments of time stitched with care,
Embraces born from the air.

Imagine the magic, where eyes align,
In unexpected places, love will shine.
Each meeting crafted by fate's own hand,
Infinite moments, a life so grand.

The Dance of Happy Accidents

Steps misaligned, yet feet find flow,
In awkward twirls, we learn to glow.
A stumble here, a laugh unleashed,
In every blunder, joy increased.

As paths collide, a world anew,
With every turn, the skies turn blue.
Mistakes become a melody sweet,
In harmony, our hearts repeat.

Through tangled threads, a fate unfolds,
Happy accidents, stories told.
We dance through life with carefree grace,
Embracing each twist with a warm embrace.

Let laughter guide us, let go the chains,
In joyous spills, love remains.
With every misstep, a lesson learned,
In this dance of life, affection burns.

Fortuity in Hidden Moments

In quiet corners, fate appears,
Whispers of chance among our fears.
A second glance, a subtle spark,
Where time stands still, a light in the dark.

Fortune hides in shadows deep,
In those still moments, secrets keep.
A chance encounter on a rainy street,
The universe conspires, our hearts meet.

Subtle signs that twist and weave,
In hidden moments, we believe.
Each fleeting glance, a story spun,
In serendipity's embrace, we've won.

Let's seize the day, with hearts so bold,
In uncharted paths, our tales unfold.
Fortuity sings in the silent glide,
In hidden moments, love won't hide.

Unexpected Blossoms of Affection

In winter's chill, a flower blooms,
Breaking through where silence looms.
From barren earth, colors arise,
Awakening dreams beneath the skies.

A smile exchanged, petals unfurl,
In hesitant hearts, emotions swirl.
From simple kindness, bonds begin,
Unexpected love, where we fit in.

Through cracks in stone, new life fights,
In every shadow, warmth ignites.
Amidst the chaos, beauty thrives,
In time's embrace, our spirit drives.

So let us cherish every surprise,
In uncharted gardens, love will rise.
Unexpected blossoms of affection bloom,
In the heart's quiet way, dispelling gloom.

The Coincidence of One Heart

When two souls collide in the night,
A spark ignites, a shared delight.
Whispers of fate in every glance,
Moments that weave a serendipitous dance.

Through shadows and light, they find their way,
In laughter and silence, they choose to stay.
A chance meeting, yet none can ignore,
The beautiful truth of one heart's core.

As stars align in the velvet sky,
A tapestry woven, you and I.
In every heartbeat, a rhythm divine,
Coincidences mold, our hearts entwine.

Not merely by luck, but a gentle thread,
We walk paths paved where love has led.
In the dance of existence, we play our part,
Forever connected, the coincidence of heart.

Mending with the Unexpected

Through cracks in the armor, light starts to seep,
Healing begins, when we finally weep.
A stranger's kind word, a gentle embrace,
The unexpected gifts time cannot erase.

In moments of doubt, when we feel so small,
A flicker of hope can break down the wall.
When life's tangled threads begin to unwind,
In the chaos, a treasure we often can't find.

Through paths unforeseen, we stumble and bend,
New chapters emerge, as the old ones end.
Embracing the mess, we discover the art,
Of mending our lives, piece by piece, heart by heart.

So let the winds bring what they may,
For in every storm, there's a brighter day.
Unexpected blessings teach us to thrive,
Mending our spirits, feeling alive.

Collecting Unforeseen Joys

In tiny moments, joy starts to bloom,
A child's laughter, dispelling the gloom.
The warmth of the sun on a chilly morning,
Unseen treasures in life keep on adorning.

A random smile from a stranger nearby,
Unexpected kindness makes the heart fly.
In simple things, we find delight,
Collecting these joys, our spirits ignite.

The scent of fresh rain, a lover's sigh,
In fleeting seconds, we learn to fly.
Nature's whispers and friendships that grow,
In unforeseen joys, our hearts overflow.

So gather these moments, let them unfold,
For life's sweetest stories are quietly told.
When we cherish the little, the big skies soar,
In collecting joys, we're forever rich at the core.

Timeless Encounters

In a crowded room, our eyes meet once more,
A connection ignited that time can't ignore.
Each laugh we share, a thread of the past,
In timeless encounters, our shadows are cast.

Old stories linger on lips slightly curved,
Memories dancing, patiently preserved.
With every heartbeat that echoes in space,
We find our way back to a familiar place.

Like seasons that change yet return once again,
In the weave of our lives, there's no need for pen.
For love knows no boundaries, no end to its flight,
In timeless encounters, everything feels right.

So let the moments unfold with grace,
In the dance of existence, we find our place.
United by time, and threads yet unknown,
In encounters eternal, we are never alone.

Tides of Joyful Surprise

Waves crash gently on the shore,
Each moment whispers, 'There's more.'
Seashells glisten in the sun,
Joyful surprises have begun.

Clouds drift softly across the blue,
Breezes dance, revealing the new.
Laughter echoes, hearts awake,
Every step, a joyful break.

Footprints track the sand's embrace,
New horizons, a welcoming space.
As the tide rolls in and out,
Wonder blooms, replacing doubt.

In the twilight, colors swirl,
Life's a gift, a precious pearl.
With each tide, a fresh delight,
Surprises waiting, day and night.

The Joy of Unwritten Stories

Pages blank, the tales untold,
Imagination begins to unfold.
Each thought a potential dream,
Creating worlds that brightly gleam.

Characters dance upon the page,
Living freely, breaking the cage.
Every moment, new paths arise,
In unwritten stories, joy lies.

The pen awaits, a vessel of fate,
Whispers of wonder that can't wait.
With each stroke, echoes of cheer,
The beauty of tales, forever near.

Time is paused, the heart ignites,
In the silence, excitement lights.
The joy of stories shining bright,
Awaits the dawn, ignites the night.

Spirals of Fortunate Flukes

Serendipity swirls around,
In the chaos, joy is found.
Fortunate flukes lead the way,
Brightening even the dullest day.

Curves and bends in life's great dance,
Unexpected gifts, a second chance.
Happy accidents bless the road,
In each twist, a light bestowed.

With every turn, delight ignites,
Surprises bloom in sudden heights.
Luck's gentle hand guides the path,
Filling hearts with spontaneous laughs.

Winding ways and whispered chances,
Life's rich tapestry enhances.
In swirling spirals, magic weaves,
Fortunate flukes, in joy, believe.

A Canvas of Blissful Coincidence

Brushstrokes wild, colors collide,
Life's canvas where dreams reside.
Each splash a moment, fate's embrace,
Blissful coincidences, we trace.

Patterns formed from chance alone,
Artistry in the unknown.
Every hue a precious find,
In this creation, hearts combined.

The beauty lies in the unplanned,
In the mess, we understand.
Serendipity paints with flair,
A tapestry, love in the air.

So let the colors bleed and blend,
In this masterpiece, we transcend.
Life's canvas, a joyful parade,
Blissful coincidences displayed.

Hearts Colliding at Random

Beneath the careless stars they meet,
Waves of laughter in the night,
Two souls, a spark, a hearth, a beat,
A glance that feels so right.

In crowded rooms where silence hums,
Eyes dance like flickering flame,
Moments flash, the chaos drums,
Each heart knows the other's name.

A whisper shared, a secret sought,
Paths intertwine without a plan,
In this wild world, love's thread is caught,
Souls collide, they take their stand.

With every turn, a chance to feel,
With every breath, a bond that grows,
In random moments, hearts reveal,
Connections formed where no one goes.

The Serene Art of Unplanned Moments

A morning breeze, the sun climbs high,
Unexpected smiles break through,
Life's beauty found in a gentle sigh,
As dreams unfold anew.

Stumbles lead to paths untrod,
Each twist and turn, a gift bestowed,
In chaos, find the hand of God,
Where mysteries and magic flowed.

Laughter echoes through the trees,
Unfolding stories in the air,
Each heartbeat whispers, brings such ease,
In moments caught, a world laid bare.

Amidst the rush, the mind's delight,
In stillness, treasures often play,
The simple joys, soft and light,
In unplanned hours, we find our way.

Hidden Joys Along the Way

A fleeting glance, a kind hello,
The warmth of hands shared on a street,
In quiet corners, joy can grow,
Small moments make life sweet.

In puddles deep, reflections shine,
Each step reveals a hidden grace,
Nature's whispers, soft as wine,
A heart that finds its rightful place.

The laughter of a child at play,
The rustle of leaves, a gentle sigh,
With each soft dawn, the golden ray,
Hidden joys, they never lie.

As we wander, pause to see,
The treasures tucked in every day,
In life's embrace, so wild and free,
Hidden joys along the way.

Discoveries in the Quiet

In tranquil spaces, thoughts take flight,
Whispers echo, dreams reside,
In stillness, there's a subtle light,
Where secrets and reflections hide.

The world slows down, a gentle breath,
Moments linger, time bends slow,
In the hush, there's life, not death,
Wisdom blooms, like flowers grow.

Each silent pause, a chance to know,
The beauty held in soft refrain,
In quietude, the heart can show,
The art of love, the dance of pain.

Discoveries in layers deep,
Reveal themselves without a sound,
In quiet corners, we can leap,
To find the joy that's all around.